T0079705

Newton
and the Club of Astronomers

I do not know what I may appear to the world, but to myself I seem to have been only like a boy playing on the sea-shore, and diverting myself in now and then finding a smoother pebble or a prettier shell than ordinary, whilst the great ocean of truth lay all undiscovered before me.

Sir Isaac Newton

Newton
and the Club of Astronomers

Narrated by
Marion Kadi and Abram Kaplan

Illustrated by
Tatiana Boyko

Translated by
Jordan Lee Schnee

Plato & Co.
diaphanes

"Wow!" shouted the scholar Isaac Newton, bounding out of his house one beautiful July morning in 1682.

During the night, his neighbor's cat had been multiplied by seven. Each cat was a different color. There was a red cat, an orange cat; another was yellow, a green one, a blue one, an indigo, and a purple one. That was a lot of cats for just one neighbor.

But when Newton took off his glasses, the seven felines recomposed into a single cat. The animal was snuffling in the morning dew. Newton decided to continue his walk in the streets of Cambridge, slipping his strange glasses back on.

They weren't really glasses, they were five-sided glass prisms which faced out of a frame that Newton wore behind his ears. He was the only one that century who wore glasses this way. The prisms broke down white light passing through them into seven colors. Obviously, wearing the glasses gave the scientist a very unusual appearance, and Cambridge's inhabitants could not keep themselves from stopping as he went by. Isaac Newton's movements were unpredictable, and it often happened that he would bump into people. He did not apologize, just exclaimed "Ooh!" and "Ah!" in delight when he saw them. Sometimes he stuck out his hand and grabbed a nose, an earring, a hat, a dog's ear. The residents of Cambridge thought he was very annoying, while he marveled at the swirling rainbows he saw appear in their hair.

Reaching the end of his stroll at the top of a hill, Newton exchanged his bifocals for a spyglass, which he pointed into the distance. Cambridge's narrow houses jostled each other in device's viewfinder.

"Look at that, Mrs. Stillingfleet is drinking tea. I've got no idea what everyone sees in that new drink. And there," he said, turning on his heels, "there's stern Mr. Chillingworth stuffing himself with porridge. Fascinating!"

He pointed the spyglass at the library and encountered another eye, glued to the eyepiece of a telescope.

"Oh heavens, I'm being watched!"

Newton was so surprised that he dropped his spyglass. It rolled down the hill, disappearing into tall grass. The scholar ran down the slope in pursuit, stopping short at the edge of a hole.

"Oh no!" he cried, smacking his forehead.

He had made the small telescope himself by hand. It was the apple of his eye.

Determined to get his device back, he held his nose, closed his eyes, and jumped in the hole.

Newton fell and fell, faster and faster! The sides of his jacket flapped like wings above his head. Soon he could not see anything anymore.

Gradually the temperature rose, and soon the darkness glowed red.

"Mercy, I'm here in hell!"

The scientist was sweating bullets. He was so hot that his thoughts evaporated as soon as they formed.

Soon he thought nothing at all.

When he came to his senses, he was still falling, but less quickly.

"I'm slowing down! I'm slowing down!"

A puff of fresh air came to him. Then he saw a tiny blue dot. It was far, far away at the bottom of the hole.

"The blue of the sky! Is it possible that I've gone through the Earth?"
He felt as proud as if he had dug the tunnel with his own hands.

The blue dot was getting bigger. Newton could make out a small shadow watching him come out of the depths.
He waved.

"Hello! Hello!"
But the other did not answer.

"How strange, that silhouette looks like the engravings of Pinguinus that I saw in the Royal Society's journal..."

As he approached the end of the tunnel, Newton exclaimed:

"But this Pinguinus has my spyglass! Give me back my telescope, Pinguinus!"

But then Newton slowed to a stop, and the next moment he was being drawn backwards.

"Help! Grab my hand!" he shouted to the penguin.

Of course, the animal did not lift a feather, and Newton felt himself get pulled faster and faster into the darkness.

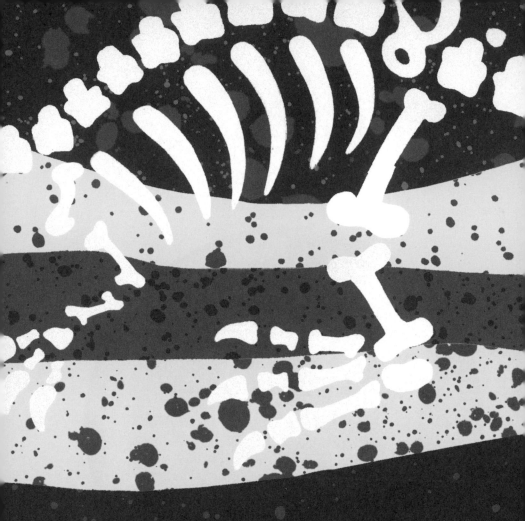

"Just my luck, here I am back in hell."
He scratched his nose.

"My spyglass fell out onto the other side. Why didn't I? I
accelerated until the center of the Earth, then I lost speed until
I came to a complete stop. That means I didn't travel the exact
distance to and from the center."

Across the tunnel, fossils embedded in the wall momentarily
distracted his attention.

"Wow look at that! There are even starfish. This is definitely proof that the Earth used to be covered in water."

At that moment raindrops started falling on him.

"And there's proof that I'm close to England!"

When he felt himself start slowing down, he grew worried.

"What if I get stuck in this tunnel like a pendulum, oscillating from one pole to the other until I come to rest in the center of the Earth forever? I would definitely have to go without pudding, and the world would have to go without my genius!"

15

Newton grabbed hold of a root, found a foothold, and began climbing the wall. When he hoisted himself out of the tunnel, completely covered in dirt, the sun was approaching the horizon.

"I'll be back!" he called in the direction of the hole. "And I'll take back what's mine!"

Then he hurried towards town.

That summer, a group of kids had been amusing themselves with slingshots. Cambridge's residents, naturally, were not amused. The children harvested their ammunition from the trees: cherries and plums, picking the ripest fruits they could find. Passers-by constantly found their clothes getting stained red and purple. It got so bad that the well-informed were now going out in raincoats.

Newton arrived at his house examining the age-old lint that was caught in the folds of his jacket.

"Maybe I should look at this under the microscope..."

But before he had time to open the door, the slingshoteers peeked over a wall and... Pow! A volley of cherries splattered his clothes.

"Gottcha!" shouted children's voices.

Newton turned to his assailants, waited for an instant, cracked a toothy grin, then sprinted off in the opposite direction.

The children, who had expected to be chased, looked at each other in utter confusion.

Newton was running to his friend Edmond Halley's house, eager to share the idea that had just come to him with the barrage of cherries.

"At this hour, he'll definitely be in his observatory," he thought to himself.

Halley's house was certainly a strange one. It consisted of a single room with a tower stuck in the middle of it that was much higher than the church belfry.

Halley shared Newton's passion for the stars. He spent his nights watching comets, his eye glued to his telescope. With the other eye, he would read mathematics and astronomy treatises, or just sleep.

When he did not find his friend on the ground floor, Newton rushed up the dark, twisted staircase to the tower. Halley, who was afraid of heights, had not wanted windows.

When Newton appeared on the balcony, covered in stains and dirt, the master of the house exclaimed:

"What a state you're in, Isaac my friend! Did you get into a fight?"

"Definitely! With gravity!"

"So you fell?"

"Yes, and not just a short way! I fell from one side of the Earth to the other. And I lost my spyglass."

Halley, getting vertigo just listening to Newton's story, went pale and gripped his chair tightly, fanning himself with a meteorological chart.

"If I want to get my spyglass back, I'm going to have to be like it," explained Newton. "I have to pick up speed before I enter the tunnel. Could you help me build… some kind of giant slingshot?"

A few months earlier, the two friends had constructed a cosmic clock that told both the time and the position of the planets with great precision. It was a very useful device, which, alas, weighed three tons. So they had needed to build an even bigger contraption just to move it.

This time they would have an even larger mechanical success. Getting to work that very night, they were able to draw up plans for a kind of giant catapult aimed at the ground and build the parts. At dawn they put it together beside the hillock where Newton's precious telescope had disappeared. After limbering up, he climbed into the basket and announced he was ready to go.

Halley set the machine to its maximum tension and started the countdown:
"Three, two, one … Bon voyage Isaac!"

But Newton did not hear that, he had already been shot deep into the guts of the Earth, and there was an awful whistling in his ears. A few minutes later, the South Pole's blue sky shone at the end of the tunnel. Newton came at the penguin, who was still in the same spot as before.

"That's mine!" roared Newton, snatching his spyglass from the animal's paws as he passed. He kept flying like an arrow, like a comet, like someone who is nowhere near stopping.

Bowled over on its back, the penguin watched Newton disappear into the sky, stunned by what had just happened.

Newton saw the Earth getting smaller beneath him.
"This is not at all what I had in mind," he admitted to himself.

He looked around, admiring the star-pricked vault for a long
while.

"Well, there's a constellation that I've never seen before. It looks like a frog! I'll have to talk to Halley about that one."

But when he looked back down at his feet, he shouted in surprise.

"The Earth is gone! Earth has deserted me!"

It didn't take long for him to realize that the Earth was behind his back.

"That's strange," he murmured, "strange indeed. It was here and now it's there. What's going on?"

He suspected the Earth had taken advantage of his inattention to revolve around him, then he remembered the penguin. For a moment, the animal had clung to the telescope as Newton was trying to tear it away. This resistance, however brief, had been enough to deflect Newton's trajectory.

"So it was me who changed direction. But where am I going then? And when will I fall back down? Okay, okay don't panic. Everything that rises always falls back to Earth. Just a little patience."

But Newton did not fall back down, and he was starting to get chilly.

"Halley's going to be worried that I'm not back."

Newton sighed; space seemed empty to him now, desolate.

He looked at the Earth, time went by. Between the huge expanses of water, he saw countries that he had never been to, and ones he would probably never visit. Finally, he recognized the English countryside and knew that he had circled the globe.

"I've become a satellite. I'm going to be stuck here forever," he thought sadly. "How long is it going to take Halley to track my orbit and plot me in his astronomy books along with the Moon?"

He saw it shining, far off.

"The Moon revolves around the Earth too. The same force is keeping it from heading off straight into the infinity of space as me."

Newton felt tired. He closed his eyes and stretched out his arms and legs like a starfish.

A foghorn's blast woke him with a start. Newton watched a kind of rowboat come out of the constellation Taurus and move towards him.

"Move it! Can't you see you're in our way?" a young man in a giant curly wig shouted at him.

"I'm not in your way, you're in mine!" answered Newton.

A second figure sitting at the stern of the small vessel, took in the oars and then turned around. He seemed to be quite a bit older. He had an ample nose, a small mustache, and bulging eyes. Newton recognized him immediately:

"Descartes? Mr. Descartes, is that you?"

The young man with the curly wig turned to his companion: "You know this guy?"

"Never seen him. To whom do we owe the pleasure?"

"I'm Isaac Newton, a mathematician from England. I've read all of your books Mr. Descartes!"

"That's great, but did you understand them?" replied Descartes, laughing. "I'm sure you know my young friend too," he added.

He brought the lantern that was hanging at the back of the boat to his companion's face:

"Please allow me to introduce Gottfried Wilhelm Leibniz."

Newton nodded.

"Ah, of course, Leibniz, I saw your calculating machine when I was in London. Where are you going?

"Wherever the whirlpool takes us," said Descartes.

"What whirlpool?"

"The one that flows around the universe, of course! The same one that carries the Earth around the Sun."

"I don't see any whirlpool," said Newton, looking around.

He did a few strokes of breaststroke and added:

"I don't feel any swirling, do you?"

"The whirlpool is here, but you can't see it with the naked eye. It's made up of particles that are too small to see," Descartes explained.

"So this whirlpool is just a hypothesis," Newton said.
Leibniz nodded vigorously.
"Science needs hypotheses to progress. Observation isn't enough."
"The Moon can't orbit on its own," Descartes added. Dangling his hand off the side of the boat, as if to feel the current, he said:
"Without the whirlpool, it would move in a straight line."

"I agree with you," said Newton. "The Moon can't orbit on its own, but, if I may, it seems to me that the force that makes it orbit is the same one that draws objects towards the center of the Earth. Gravitational force!"

"And how is this gravitational force exerted?" asked Leibniz.
"Remotely."
"But how, and why?
"Those aren't the questions I'm trying to answer at the
moment. Me, I don't make hypotheses," he added with a wink.
"Well how can you make any discoveries with those methods?"
exclaimed Leibniz.
"It's simple. I follow a line of reasoning. That helps bridle
in imagination and avoid fantastical speculations that are a
menace to us all, like that crackpot whirlpool idea."

"And what's the line of reasoning?" asked Descartes.

"If I observe two phenomena that are similar, then they have the same cause," said Newton with pride. "For example, the Earth revolves around the Sun. Jupiter does too. I have observed that the attracting force exerted upon each planet by the Sun decreases with the square of the distance separating them. So it must be the same force that's making Earth and Jupiter orbit— and of course, Mars, Venus and all the other planets too."

"Earth exerts force on the Moon," continued Newton. "Why doesn't it exert force on the Sun? If gravity is a reciprocal force, then all the celestial bodies—the Moon! The Earth! The Sun!—exert it upon each other. How am I going to be able to confirm that one?" he asked.

"My dear friend, aren't you dangerously close to formulating a hypothesis?" Leibniz asked wickedly.

"Come ride in our boat instead of just going around us,"
Descartes added.

Newton looked around.
"I'm revolving around you! Then you exert a gravitational force
upon me! There's the proof I was waiting for! All bodies attract
all other bodies!"

Descartes held out a hand to hoist Newton up into the vessel.

Sitting at the bow of the boat beside Leibniz, Newton solemnly announced:

"Outer space is quite conducive to genius ideas."

"Your system seems very unstable to me," Leibniz objected. "Tell me why the planets don't crash into the Sun, if they are attracted by its gravitational force."

"The Creator of the universe obviously adjusts their trajectories," replied Newton.

"Well that's exactly what seems doubtful. If God were a watchmaker, he wouldn't make a watch that he had to reset all of the time. He would create a perfect watch that would be set once and forever."

"Your watchmaker God, my dear Leibniz, would let the mechanism go by itself. But God didn't create the universe and then abandon it to its own devices. On the contrary, every second he is maintaining the order of his creation."

The rocking boat along with the conversation made Descartes feel sick. He did not like arguments. According to him, philosophical truths were not objects of discussion; they were clear and evident; they made everyone agree.

"The members of the club would be delighted to hear your theories," he grumbled.
"The club?" asked Newton, startled.
"All the good astronomers who are on the Moon have a club."

"The Club of Astronomers! I thought that was a myth!"

"No, it's very real," replied Leibniz, "we just came from there.
Did you think we'd gone for a row in space looking for a tavern?"

Descartes leaned over the gunwale.
"If we push you hard enough, my dear Newton, maybe you can join
the club."
"Well I'm not sure that..."

But Leibniz had already shoved Newton out of the boat.

"Are you sure that's the Moon?" he shouted as he drifted off.
"I don't recognize any of the formations I usually see."

"That's because you're looking at the dark side, the one that's
impossible to see from the Earth! Say 'Hi' to the members of the
club for us!"

The Moon quickly grew closer and closer. Newton felt heavier and heavier. The dust kicked up by his fall fell slowly around him. He was in the middle of a huge crater.

"Wait, it's dry down here! Where are the seas that everyone talks about in the selenography books?"

When he got up, he floated a few yards into the air, before coming back down in the same spot. Taking a step, he again bounced several yards ahead.

"My word, I have to relearn how to walk!"

And that is what he did.

He had not gone very far when he noticed a print in the dust. "Just one print, and it's fresh. Apparently the creature who made it makes huge leaps."

To his great surprise, it was a young woman who was waiting for him a little way ahead. She was dressed in an ancient fashion.
"Did you see my wings?" she asked him, as if it were the most natural thing in the world.
"Your wings?"
"Yes, my wings of fire."
"No, I didn't see them. But I'm new on the Moon.
The young woman was obviously disappointed.
"If you come back here in a few centuries, you'll see your footprints," she said.
"Tracks never fade on the Moon, there's no wind."
"I ... I came to meet the members of the Club of Astronomers," put in Newton, confused.
"Of course," she said, "I'll drive you."

On the way she told him, "A long time ago I tried to draw a map of the Earth, but I didn't have enough perspective. I wasn't sure I hadn't missed a sea or a continent. So it occurred to me to fly the furthest away that I could from the center of the World."

"The Earth isn't the center of the World," replied Newton, for lack of something better to say.

"You talk like the others," said the young woman, chuckling. "They also say that the Sun's the center of the World."

"They're right. On the Earth and on the Moon, you can't tell that you're revolving around the Sun; but when you travel from one to the other, you can see it easily."

"What about you? Who are you?" Newton asked shyly.
"My name is Ptolemy," said the young woman with smiling eyes.

They came to a stop in front of a narrow red brick house with stepped gables. The façade was adorned with stained glass and molding. "None Shall Pass Unless They Are an Astronomer" read the inscription on the pediment. Ptolemy knocked on the door. Right away, a man stuck his head through the window next to it.

"Come in through here—the dog ate the key."

The window opened onto a large lounge. All of the furniture, with the exception of a few armchairs, had been pushed against the walls. A meteorite the size of an elephant occupied the center of the room. It was covered in veins of a peculiar metal.

"Canon Nicolaus Copernicus," said the man, introducing himself.

"I'm Isaac Newton; astronomer, mathematician, philosopher, physicist, theologian. Pray tell, how did this house get here?"

"Please, take a seat," said Copernicus.

He picked up a little dog that was sleeping on one of the armchairs and put it on his lap.

"The house came with me. I was sitting in this very armchair, contemplating the fog over the Vistula that was preventing my observations. At the height of my frustration, I imagined what the movement of the planets would look like from the Sun. At the time, I was sure that the Earth was the center of the universe, then suddenly..."

Copernicus closed his eyes.

Geocentrism

"Suddenly, I saw the Earth going by my window. I thought I had been transported to the Sun, but to my great surprise, when I went outside I saw it shining in the sky. I was on the Moon! The center always seems like wherever you are, right?" He said, with a friendly smile towards Ptolemy.

"If it always feels like we're at the center, then how can we know what the true midpoint is?" She murmured.

"The most elegant physical model should be chosen. If the Sun is the center of the World, the planet's orbits are simple and harmonious, very round. If you put the Earth in the center, their trajectories become messy."

"My world system is not messy, it's complex," said Ptolemy, offended.

The crash of breaking glass made the little dog jump.

Copernicus looked up and called out:
"Kepler, is that you?"

The shaggy-haired scholar Johannes Kepler came hurtling down the stairs.

"The planet's trajectories around the Sun are not round, Copernicus! I've explained it to you ten times, none of the measurements are accurate unless the orbits are slightly elliptical. When I heard you say that, I broke my lens. The one I've been polishing for months!" He pouted.

To console him, Newton pulled the five-sided glasses from his pocket. Kepler examined them.
"These glass prisms are beautifully cut," he announced.

He perched the glasses on his nose and looked at a candle's flame in wonder. Newton then turned to Copernicus. "Do you welcome many astronomers to your home?"

"Yes indeed, but how many depends on how you count the ones who come from the future: the latest arrival, for example, is a remarkable young man by the name of Steven Hawking. He'll be born in 1942. Galileo's the one who keeps the list up to date, you'll find him just next door in his construction site." "What's he building?" "An observation tower, of course."

Guided by Kepler, who never took off his new glasses, Newton and Ptolemy came back out through the window, leaving the club's headquarters. They made a few leaps and bounds, stopping at the edge of a small crater. Down below, Galileo was lifting stones that were far larger than he was.

"Was there water here before?" Asked Newton.
"No," answered Kepler. "We've searched extensively but we haven't found water. This crater is from a meteor strike. The one we keep in the lounge."

Galileo pitched the boulders onto the top of his tower, stopping occasionally to survey the pile with his telescope.
"Is everyone stronger on the Moon?" Newton wondered.

He lifted up a rock with the tip of his foot, caught it gracefully, then threw it a great distance.

"45 degrees, the perfect angle on Earth!" Galileo said to his visitors, obviously delighted to receive them. "But to equal the meteor strike," he told them, "you've got to aim higher!"

"Galileo worked as an engineer for the Venetian Arsenal," explained Ptolemy. "He's a great specialist in projectile ballistics. He can predict the path of a body in motion with incredible precision. He came here by way of a cannon whose angle and power he calculated."

Galileo, who was looking for an audience, had carved bleachers into the crater walls. The astronomers hopped down from step to step to reach him.

"It reminds me of the amphitheaters from my childhood," said Ptolemy.

Galileo rubbed his dusty hands together.

"I noticed that objects fall more slowly on the Moon than on Earth. I intend to discover why by measuring the descents of things that I drop from the top of this observation tower."

"If you don't mind me saying," Newton said, "I would posit that objects fall more slowly on the Moon because they weigh less."

"That's a ridiculous theory," answered Galileo. "On Earth, all objects fall at the same speed, no matter what they weigh. When I dropped a little pillow and a big cannonball from the top of the tower of Pisa they hit the ground at exactly the same time."

"The speed at which objects fall has nothing to do with their mass, but with their weight," Newton said.

Galileo opened his eyes wide because he did not know the difference between "mass" and "weight"—and rightly so, as Newton had just invented it.

"Take this little pebble," said Newton. "I call the amount of matter that composes this pebble its "mass." The force of attraction that the Moon exerts on it is its "weight." Its mass, the quantity of matter in the pebble, will never change. But if it were on the Earth right now, its weight would be greater, because the Earth exerts a greater force of attraction on the object than the Moon does."

"And why is that?" Asked Galileo.

"Because the Earth's mass is larger. If this rock were on the Sun, it would be even heavier."

"And what about us?" Kepler asked, cutting in.

"We would definitely be so heavy that we wouldn't even be able to stand up."

Newton's explanations whipped Galileo into a veritable euphoria.

"Venerable Newton, as is custom at the court of the Medicis, let me make a gift to you of my telescope, and all the stars that you can see with it."

"Honorable Galileo, I give to you this pebble, and my theory of gravitation that goes with it."

"Galileo gives stars to everyone," whispered Ptolemy. "Last time, he gave them to Nasir al-Din al-Tusi, who lives in the neighboring crater with some other astronomers. He got here a long time ago."

"First woman on the Moon ..." Newton bowed.

"I'm the only one who has circumnavigated it in all directions," she replied. "But now, I'm observing the Earth so I can finish the geography book that I started writing here. I was curious to see what was on the opposite side of my country, Egypt."

"Water, certainly?"

"Yes, that's what I had conjectured. But I also discovered a new continent! Kepler wanted to call it America, but I named it Atlantis."

"I flew over those lands before coming here. They are not so different from England. Gravitation effects them in the same way," said Newton.

Copernicus approached with long, slow strides, gesticulating wildly, his little dog under his arm.

"I think he's trying to tell us something," Kepler said.

"Look up there!" shouted Copernicus. "Something's headed our way!"

"Everybody take cover! It's going to fall on us, I'm certain," lamented Kepler, hiding himself behind Ptolemy.

Newton and Galileo extended their telescopes.

"It's a comet!" announced Newton.

"I see it too," said Galileo. "It's quite a beautiful comet. It has a very flamboyant hairstyle."

"Can't you see it's huge? Soon it's going to strike the Moon," moaned Kepler.

Ptolemy shrugged.

"When I arrived on the Moon, every day it was raining comets, and I had no telescope to see them coming."

"I'm scared, I'm scared," Kepler was repeating.

"Don't worry," said Galileo. This comet is going to pass close to the Moon, but it won't hit us."
"Galileo, you're a specialist in cannonballs, not comets," commented Copernicus.
"Wait, someone's on the comet!" exclaimed Galileo.
"Do you see him too, Newton?"
"It's Halley!" He cried, "He's coming to get me!"

The comet skimmed past the Moon. Halley threw down a long rope that everyone grabbed hold of.

With a great effort, Newton, who was the first to wrap the rope around his leg, managed to climb up to the icy surface of the comet. He looked down behind him: Copernicus, who was climbing with his dog under his arm, was slowing the rest of the troop's ascent.

Newton came through a cloud of dust and saw Halley's face. The two friends embraced each other heartily.
"But how did you know I was on the Moon?" exclaimed Newton.

"The night of your departure, while watching the stars, I saw you floating in the sky. You soon disappeared behind the Moon. I was worried! When this comet passed near the Earth, I was able to calculate its path, and I discovered that it was heading for the Moon. Right away, I went looking for the longest rope I could find, and I asked the children of Cambridge to shoot me onto the comet with our catapult… the Newton Thrower."

Newton smiled.
"My friend, I know your knees go wobbly as soon as you get on a chair, so I can't imagine what it's like for you here!"

"I needed a change of scenery. My tower has been invaded by a penguin who now prevents me from observing the stars with my telescope. I've tried everything to get rid of him, but he's stubborn."

The Antarctic penguin had jumped into the hole and gone through to Cambridge. He had been looking for a telescope ever since Newton had retrieved his spyglass, so he set his sights on Halley's observatory.

"So, what about the Moon?" asked Halley, hungry for details. "It's not as dry as you would think. There are mostly just rocks, but..."
Newton turned towards the horde of out-of-breath astronomers who were coming over to join them.
"Halley my man, let me introduce you some fellow astronomers; this is Mr. Copernicus, Galileo, and Kepler, and this is Ms. Ptolemy."

"It's a good thing this comet didn't fall on our heads," said Galileo, looking around. "It's huge."

"It was prettier from a distance," said Ptolemy. "Up close it's like a big, dirty snowball."

Kepler had put Newton's glasses back on, and was walking across the icy surface in little steps.

"No, it's quite beautiful," he declared. "It shines with a million rainbows. But it's true that it's a bit cold."

"It's going to heat up," announced Copernicus. "We're headed for the Sun."

"That's right. This comet is orbiting our star. We'll come back past the Earth in a little over 75 years," explained Halley.

"Well that gives us some time to get to know each other," said Isaac Newton with a smile.

French Edition:

Newton et la confrérie des astronomes

Raconté par Marion Kadi et Abram Kaplan

Illustré par Tatiana Boyko

Design : Yohanna Nguyen et Avril du Payrat

© Les petits Platons, Paris 2018

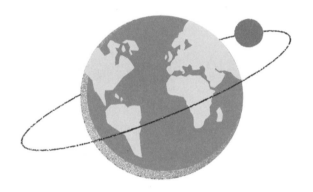

First edition

ISBN 978-3-0358-0140-8

© DIAPHANES, Zurich 2019

www.diaphanes.com

Layout: 2edit, Zurich

Printed and bound in Germany